This book is dedicated to all the people who encouraged me to compile all the work into an unconventional and practical guide to learning and mastering the Azure ARM Templates.

About the Author

Aman Sharma is Microsoft Azure MVP and is currently working as Principal Technical Consultant with Infront Consulting Group for the Private and Public cloud, where he architects and designs various solutions around Microsoft Azure and related technologies. He ensures the security in the design along with the incorporation of best practices leveraging various Azure technologies to their full potential.

Aman is passionate about technology and how it can change the way we experience life on day to day basis. He comes from a development background and has led the development of various products around Azure. He works with both IaaS and PaaS features of Azure. He has been building enterprise solutions around Azure Cost and Performance Optimizations, Azure Billing & Chargeback, Enterprise Datacenter Management solutions, etc.

Aman has around 10 years of industry experience. Prior to joining Infront, he was part of Microsoft for around 5 years. Aman currently lives in Greater Toronto Area (GTA), Canada.

His contact information can be found as below:

 20aman@gmail.com

 http://HarvestingClouds.com

 @20aman

 https://ca.linkedin.com/in/20aman

Contents

◆ ◆ ◆

INTRODUCTION – ARM TEMPLATES

Azure Resource Manager (ARM) Template is a JavaScript Object Notation (JSON) file that defines one or more resources to deploy to a resource group. It also defines the dependencies between the deployed resources. The template can be used to deploy the resources consistently and repeatedly.

ARM Templates can be used for the deployment of resources on both Azure and Azure Stack. Using these templates for all deployments provides you with various **benefits** including:

- **Declarative Deployment** – All you need to do is declare what you need to deploy. You don't need to create any complex rules or write lengthy scripts.
- **Idempotency** – You can deploy the same template over and over again without affecting the current resources.
- **Predictability** - Using Templates you can have accurate predictability when performing large deployments. You reduce any manual errors.
- **Repetition without Errors** - You can deploy the same infrastructure over and over again (e.g. in Dev-test environments and then in production).

In this book, we will try to decode and understand the ARM Templates in a practical approach.

CHAPTER 1 - JSON 101 FOR IT ADMINISTRATORS

A quick primer on JSON

Azure Resource Manager (ARM) templates are written in JSON or **JavaScript Object Notation**. To understand ARM templates, you need to understand few quick basics about JSON. These will enable you to lay a great foundation which will enable you to understand ARM templates very easily.

JSON or JavaScript Object Notation (pronounce like "Jay-son") is a text-based data format that's designed to be human-readable, lightweight, and easy to transmit between a server and a web client. Its syntax is derived from JavaScript. Think of this as an even more compact version of XML files.

JSON is a popular notation for transmitting data through RESTful web services. The official internet media type for JSON is application/json, and JSON files typically have a .json extension.

To understand JSON we need to understand **3 main components**. These components are like building blocks, using which you can build very complex JSON files.

1. Objects

Objects are the heart of JSON. Object denotes a real-life object, e.g. an Employee. Just like a real-life object, these have various properties and a value for each of these properties. E.g. An Employee will have Name property with value as John. Further, an employee object can have various another properties like Age, Salary, Department etc. So to denote an object in JSON you:

- One object will be represented by curly brackets. It will begin from opening curly bracket i.e. { and will end at closing curly bracket i.e. }
- Denote the property and corresponding values as "key" : "value" or "property" : "value" pairs.
- You can only use double quotes for Properties as they will always be of type string

- You will have double quotes around Values if they are of string type. You will not have any quotes in case of a number or a boolean value.
- Each property will be separated from next property by a comma

Note: Each JSON file is also a single JSON object. At root level, it starts with an opening curly bracket i.e. { and will end with closing curly bracket i.e. }. There can't be any other objects at the root level. Think of this similar to how in an XML file there can be only one element at the root level.

Example Employee object is shown below:

```
{
"Name" : "John",
"Age" : 34,
"Department" : "Finance",
"Salary" : "100000",
"IsAdmin" : true
}
```

2. Arrays

Simply put, arrays are a collection of items. In JSON the **square brackets** represent an Array. E.g. An array of employees will look like below:

```
[
{
"Name" : "John",
"Age" : 34
},
{
"Name" : "Mary",
"Age" : 32
},
{
"Name" : "Matthew",
"Age" : 29
}
]
```

3. Nesting of Objects

Now things get more interesting with nesting of Objects. What Nesting means is that one object can have it property as another complex object. Don't worry if that sounds confusing. Let's understand that statement using an example. An Address where a person lives can be represented by an object. This object will look like below:

```
{
"StreetNumber" : "50",
"StreetName" : "Brian Harrison Way",
"Unit Number" : 22,
"City" : "Toronto",
```

```
    "Country" : "Canada"
    }
```

Now an Employee Object will have an Address object as one of its property (because employee needs to live somewhere). This new complex Employee object will look like below, with nested Address object as one of its property:

```
{
    "Name" : "John",
    "Age" : 34,
    "Department" : "Finance",
    "Salary" : "100000",
    "IsAdmin" : true,
    "Address" :  {
    "StreetNumber" : "50",
    "StreetName" : "Brian Harrison Way",
    "Unit Number" : 22,
    "City" : "Toronto",
    "Country" : "Canada"
    }
}
```

That's all there is to it. Now you can use these 3 components and build very complex JSON files/templates. Even the most complex template can be broken into these 3 components.

Below is a complex example with all 3 components.

```
{
    "Department": "Finance",
    "TotalEmployees": 2,
    "Employees": [
    {
    "Name": "John",
    "Age": 34,
    "Department": "Finance",
    "Salary": "100000",
    "IsAdmin": true,
    "Address": {
    "StreetNumber": "50",
    "StreetName": "Brian Harrison Way",
    "Unit Number": 22,
    "City": "Toronto",
    "Country": "Canada"
    }
    },
    {
    "Name": "John",
    "Age": 34,
    "Department": "Finance",
    "Salary": "100000",
    "IsAdmin": true,
    "Address": {
```

```
    "StreetNumber": "50",
    "StreetName": "Brian Harrison Way",
    "Unit Number": 22,
    "City": "Toronto",
    "Country": "Canada"
    }
    }
    ]
    }
```

The above JSON object denotes one department with name as Finance and total number of employees as 2. Then the "Employees" object is an array of 2 employees. Each employee object further have a complex property as Address, which is another object.

If you understood each of the 3 components, you should be able to build/understand most complex JSON files with ease.

CHAPTER 2 - WHAT IS IN AN ARM TEMPLATE

Understanding All Components

As we discussed earlier in the introduction **Azure Resource Manager (ARM) Template** is a JavaScript Object Notation (JSON) file that defines one or more resources to deploy to a resource group. It also defines the dependencies between the deployed resources.

In this chapter, we will deconstruct any basic ARM template and will understand it's various components. Any ARM Template will look like below:

```
{
"$schema": "https://schema.management.azure.com/schemas/2015-01-01/deploymentTemplate.json#",
"contentVersion": "1.0.0.0",
"parameters": {},
"variables": {},
"resources": [ {}, {} ]
}
```

Snapshot of the Template at root level, as generated via Visual Studio:

As you can see the components (or properties) of any ARM template includes:

1. Schema
2. Content Version
3. Parameters
4. Variables
5. Resources

Let's look at these in more detail.

Element name	Required	JSON Type	Description
$schema	Yes	String Value	Location of the JSON schema file that describes the version of the template language.
contentVersion	Yes	String Value	A version of the template (such as 1.2.0.20). When deploying resources using the template, this value can be used to make sure that the right template is being used.
parameters	No	JSON Object	Values that are provided by the end user (manually or via parameters file) when deployment is executed to customize resource deployment.
variables	No	JSON Object	Values that are reused multiple times in the template. You can update these values. They are different from Parameters as their value is known and they are not required as inputs from the end user.
resources	Yes	Array of Objects	Types of services that are deployed or updated in a resource group. Each JSON object in this Array denotes an Azure Resource.
outputs	No	JSON Object	Values that are returned after deployment.

Now that you know what each part is at a high level, in the next chapters, we will look at the following key components in detail, i.e.

1. Parameters
2. Variables
3. Resources
4. Outputs

1. Parameters

As mentioned earlier, parameters are the way to customize the templates, each time you deploy it to create sources in Azure. These parameters are the end-user inputs for various aspects of the template. E.g. If you are ploying an Azure Virtual Machine via an ARM Template then the name of the VM can be an input parameter. erating System type can be another parameter.

The parameters can be referred and used in other parts of the ARM Template.

1. Defining Parameters

Parameters is a one huge JSON object with multiple JSON properties. Each property is one parameter which is presented as another JSON object. Let us look at its structure at a high level.

```
"parameters": {
"parameter 1" : {},
"parameter 2" : {},
"parameter 3" : {}
}
```

E.g. If you are creating a template to deploy a Windows Virtual Machine then the parameters will look mething like below:

```
"parameters": {
"VMName" : {},
"AdminUserName" : {},
"AdminPassword" : {},
"WindowsOSVersion" : {}
}
```

Now let us look at one of the parameters. E.g. The AdminUserName parameter will look like:

```
"adminUsername": {
"type": "string",
"minLength": 1,
"metadata": {
"description": "Username for the Virtual Machine."
}
}
```

The parameter object, as shown above, has following parts:

1. **Type** – This is the data Type of the parameter.
2. **minLength** – This is the minimum length the parameter must have
3. **Metadata** – This is just to provide a description as to what the parameter means.

The **Data Types** allowed for the parameter are:

- string or secureString – any valid JSON string
- int – any valid JSON integer
- bool – any valid JSON boolean
- object – any valid JSON object
- array – any valid JSON array

A more complex parameter e.g. Windows OS Version, with few more properties, is shown below:

```
"windowsOSVersion": {
"type": "string",
"defaultValue": "2012-R2-Datacenter",
"allowedValues": [
"2008-R2-SP1",
"2012-Datacenter",
"2012-R2-Datacenter"
],
"metadata": {
"description": "The Windows version for the VM. This will pick a fully patched image of this given Windows version. Allowed
values: 2008-R2-SP1, 2012-Datacenter, 2012-R2-Datacenter."
}
}
```

It has additional properties:

1. **Default Value** – This is the default value. End User will be able to change this value when deploying the template. If no value is provided then this value is picked.
2. **Allowed Values** – This is an Array of values which are allowed for the parameter. Only value from this set is allowed as an input.

2. Using Parameters

Using parameters is easy. Wherever in your template (in variables or resources section), you want to use the value of a parameter, just use the parameter function as shown below with the name of the parameter as input enclosed in square brackets.

```
[parameters('windowsOSVersion')]
```

If the parameter value is assigned to a property, enclosing it in double quotes, as shown below:

```
"sku": "[parameters('windowsOSVersion')]"
```

3. Best Practices

- Try to always provide Default Values
- Provide metadata so that you can provide insight as to what the parameter is meant for

- Provide complete descriptive names, no matter how long.
- Use **Pascal Casing** to name your parameters. i.e. the First letter should be a small letter. Then every new word will have the first letter as a capital. No space between words. E.g. windowsOSVersion
- Use properties like minLength and Allowed values to impose restrictions. This reduces any human errors.

2. Variables

Variables are values that you either know beforehand or you can construct from the input parameters. These variables can then be reused at multiple locations in the resources section. If you later want to change the value of a variable then it automatically gets updated at all other locations. They can be used to define a resource property.

1. Defining Variables

The variable is a one huge JSON object. Each property can be one of the simple data type (like integer, bool, string etc.) or can be another complex JSON object. The general structure is as shown below:

```
"variables": {
"variable 1" : "value 1",
"variable 2" : "value 2",
"variable 3" : 1024,
"variable 4" : {}
}
```

Note that in the above example, the first 3 variables are of simple value type. The 4rth variable is however of a complex JSON object type.

Let's now check a real variables section from an actual ARM template:

```
"variables": {
"vmSize": "Standard_A2",
"virtualNetworkName": "MyVNETName",
"vnetId1": "[resourceId('Microsoft.Network/virtualNetworks', variables('virtualNetworkName'))]",
"vnetId2": "[resourceId(parameters('vNetRG'),'Microsoft.Network/virtualNetworks',parameters('virtualNetworkName'))]",
"subnetRef": "[concat(variables('vnetId'), '/subnets/', variables('subnetName'))]",
"vhdStorageName": "[concat('vhdstorage', uniqueString(resourceGroup().id))]",
"storageAccountResourceGroup": "[resourcegroup().name]",
"location": "[resourceGroup().location]",
"subscriptionId": "[subscription().subscriptionId]"
}
```

There are lots of key constructs in the above code snippet. I have tried to capture as many different constructs in this snippets as I could. Let us decode each variable one by one.

1. vmSize – Simple String
2. virtualNetworkName – Simple string name
3. vnetId1 – This uses a special function named "**resourceId**" to find out the resource ID of the virtual network. This function is invoked by using the syntax "[resourceId(Input)]" . This gets the resource ID of a resource which is defined by the Input to this. Also, note the use of another variable as an input to this.
4. vnetId2 – This also fetches the resource Id of a virtual network using "resourceId" method. Note the use of the value of a parameter in this to find out Resource Group of the existing Virtual network (parameter "vNetRG").

5. subnetRef – This variable uses another function "**concat**" in ARM template i.e. "[concat(input1,input2,...)]". This function can take many inputs and will concatenate (i.e. club together) the value of all the inputs provided. You can use parameters or another variable.
6. vhdStorageName – This also uses concat function to dynamically generate a storage name. However it uses "**resourcegroup**" function as "[resourcegroup()]". This function always returns the resource group to which you are deploying the current ARM template. Then the variable uses the id property of the resource group returned.
7. storageAccountResourceGroup – This uses the "name" property of the current resource group
8. location – This uses the "location" property of the current resource group.
9. subscriptionId – This uses the "**subscription**" function as "[subscription()]" to find out the current subscription to which the current ARM template is being deployed. Then it uses the subscription Id property of the subscription to get the required Id.

Note that these constructs are very powerful and can be used to dynamically construct your ARM template. These constructs are also known as Helper Functions and are explained in detail later.

2. Using Variables

Using variables is very easy and is similar to using parameters. In fact, you already saw the usage of variables above, while defining other variables.

You use the square parenthesis to indicate to the ARM engine to evaluate whatever is inside the parenthesis. You use the "variable" keyword and then you pass the name of the variable as input. Check the example below.

```
"storageAccountName": "[variables('storageAccountName')]"
```

3. Best Practices

Best practices are similar to the Parameters.

- Provide complete descriptive names, no matter how long.
- Use **Pascal Casing** to name your parameters. i.e. the First letter should be a small letter. Then every new word will have the first letter as a capital. No space between words. E.g. storageAccountName
- Use the constructs explained in the previous section to dynamically generate variables. This reduces any human errors.
- Anything that is used more than once and is not required to be entered by an end user, should be created as a variable. Later on, this helps by minimizing the number of places you need to change the value.

3. Resources

This is the major section of the whole ARM template. This is where you define what resources should be deployed in Azure. You also define dependencies between resources in this section.

The resources section consist of an array of JSON Objects as shown below:

```
"resources": [
{ },
{ },
]
```

Each object in the array (represented via curly braces) is an Azure resource. You can deploy multiple resource in a single ARM template. E.g. You can deploy a new Storage Account, new Virtual Network and three Virtual Machines in that virtual network within a single template. Within the object, various properties (and nested properties) are used to provide the configurations of each resource.

1. Elements

Different elements in a single resource object can be one of the following:

1. **apiVersion** – *Required* – Version of the API. e.g. "2015-06-15"
2. **type** – *Required* – Type of the resource. This value is a combination of the namespace of the resource provider and the resource type that the resource provider supports. e.g. Azure Storage Account will have type as "Microsoft.Storage/storageAccounts".
3. **name** – *Required* – Name of the resource. The name must follow URI component restrictions and also the Azure naming restrictions if any. E.g. Storage account name can only be in small letters and has to be unique.
4. **location** – Optional – Use supported geo-locations of the provided resource without any spaces. Or use the resource group's location dynamically.
5. **tags** – Optional – Tags that are associated with the resource.
6. **dependsOn** – Optional – Other resources in the same template, that the current resource being defined depends on. The dependencies between resources are evaluated and resources are deployed in the dependent order. When resources are not dependent on each other, they are attempted to be deployed in parallel. The value can be a comma-separated list of resource names or resource unique identifiers.
7. **properties** – Optional – Resource specific configuration settings. E.g. Account type property for a storage account name.
8. **resources** – Optional – Child resources that depend on the resource being defined. E.g. Extension resource for a Virtual Machine resource.

2. Examples

Let's look at two examples. First, we will take a simple resource example to deploy a storage account in Azure:

```
{
"type": "Microsoft.Storage/storageAccounts",
"name": "[variables('vhdStorageName')]",
"apiVersion": "2015-06-15",
"location": "[resourceGroup().location]",
"tags": {
"displayName": "StorageAccount",
"department" : "Finance",
```

```
    "application" : "database"
    },
    "properties": {
    "accountType": "[variables('vhdStorageType')]"
    }
    }
```

Above example will deploy a storage account with the name from "vhdStorageName" variable. It will apply 3 tags to the resource after deployment. It will use the account type (i.e. standard or premium) based on the value of the "vhdStorageType" variable. If you want to deploy 2 or more similar storage accounts, then just copy and paste the json for the resource, separated by comma. It will become another object in the Resources array.

Now let's look at a complex and larger example of deploying a single virtual machine with one extension for Diagnostics.

```
{
    "apiVersion": "2015-06-15",
    "type": "Microsoft.Compute/virtualMachines",
    "name": "[variables('vmName')]",
    "location": "[resourceGroup().location]",
    "tags": {
    "displayName": "VirtualMachine"
    },
    "dependsOn": [
    "[concat('Microsoft.Storage/storageAccounts/', variables('vhdStorageName'))]",
    "[concat('Microsoft.Network/networkInterfaces/', variables('nicName'))]"
    ],
    "properties": {
    "hardwareProfile": {
    "vmSize": "[variables('vmSize')]"
    },
    "osProfile": {
    "computerName": "[variables('vmName')]",
    "adminUsername": "[parameters('adminUsername')]",
    "adminPassword": "[parameters('adminPassword')]"
    },
    "storageProfile": {
    "imageReference": {
    "publisher": "[variables('imagePublisher')]",
    "offer": "[variables('imageOffer')]",
    "sku": "[parameters('windowsOSVersion')]",
    "version": "latest"
    },
    "osDisk": {
    "name": "osdisk",
    "vhd": {
    "uri": "[concat('http://', variables('vhdStorageName'), '.blob.core.windows.net/', variables('vhdStorageContainerName'), '/', variables('OSDiskName'), '.vhd')]"
    },
    "caching": "ReadWrite",
```

```
"createOption": "FromImage"
}
},
"networkProfile": {
"networkInterfaces": [
{
"id": "[resourceId('Microsoft.Network/networkInterfaces', variables('nicName'))]"
}
]
},
"diagnosticsProfile": {
"bootDiagnostics": {
"enabled": true,
"storageUri": "[concat('http://', variables('diagnosticsStorageAccountName'), '.blob.core.windows.net')]"
}
}
},
"resources": [
{
"type": "extensions",
"name": "Microsoft.Insights.VMDiagnosticsSettings",
"apiVersion": "2015-06-15",
"location": "[resourceGroup().location]",
"tags": {
"displayName": "AzureDiagnostics"
},
"dependsOn": [
"[concat('Microsoft.Compute/virtualMachines/', variables('vmName'))]"
],
"properties": {
"publisher": "Microsoft.Azure.Diagnostics",
"type": "IaaSDiagnostics",
"typeHandlerVersion": "1.5",
"autoUpgradeMinorVersion": true,
"settings": {
"xmlCfg": "[base64(concat(variables('wadcfgxstart'), variables('wadmetricsresourceid'), variables('wadcfgxend')))]",
"storageAccount": "[variables('diagnosticsStorageAccountName')]"
},
"protectedSettings": {
"storageAccountName": "[variables('diagnosticsStorageAccountName')]",
"storageAccountKey": "[listkeys(variables('accountid'), '2015-06-15').key1]",
"storageAccountEndPoint": "https://core.windows.net"
}
}
}
]
}
```

Note that the above code snippet defines a single virtual machine. Let us decode various sections of this complex resource:

- It begins with simple properties like apiVersion, type, name, location and tags as discussed in the previous example. These are straightforward and thus values are provided to these attributes.
- Next is the **dependsOn** section. This defines the dependency between resources. In the above example, the virtual machine resource is dependent on the storage account and a network interface, which are also defined in the template. These 2 resources will be created before the virtual machine creation/deployment. If these resources are not created in the template then it will check for the presence of these resources in the current subscription. If they are not present the template will not get deployed and will error out.
- Next are various **properties** to configure the Virtual machine, like hardware profile, os profile, storage profile, os disk, network profile, diagnostics profile etc.
- Next, we have additional **sub-resources**. These are Azure resources which will be created and linked to the current resource. Only one sub-resource is created in the above example which is an extension for VM diagnostics settings.

4. Outputs

This section is used to output any values after the deployment of the ARM Template. This can output any Ids connection strings based on the deployed resources.

This is a single JSON object with various output objects (just like Parameters. The overall JSON structure loo like below:

```json
"outputs": {
"output1" : {
"type":"string",
"value": "value1"
},
"output2" : {
"type":"string",
"value": "value2"
},
}
```

Each output object has 2 properties:

1. Type – Data type of the output
2. Value – value of the output

A real life example with look like below:

```json
"outputs": {
"adminUsername": {
"type": "string",
"value": "[parameters('adminUsername')]"
}
}
```

The above example will output the administrator Username using the parameter from the template.

CHAPTER 3 - HELPER FUNCTIONS

Make Dynamic ARM Templates

ARM Templates has various dynamic constructs called **Helper Functions** which can make your template more generic. These constructs reduce the hardcoded values in your templates. You can use the information from this chapter to make your existing templates more dynamic and start writing new templates with a much generic approach.

Let's look at the most important helper functions and their practical usage one by one.

1. Resource Id – Resource Function

You use this function to determine the ID of a resource. This is only used when the resource (whose ID is needed) is not being deployed in the current template and it already exists in Azure.
The generic syntax to use this is:

```
resourceId ([subscriptionId], [resourceGroupName], resourceType, resourceName1, [resourceName2]...)
```

Only required parameters of this helper function are resourceType and resourceName1.
These parameters are as follows:

- subscription ID – This is only needed if you want to refer a different subscription. The default value is the current subscription
- resource Group Name – Name of the resource group where the resource exists. The default is the current resource group, in which you are deploying the template
- resource Type – Type of resource including resource provider namespace
- resource Name 1 – Name of the resource
- resource Name 2 – Next resource name segment if the resource is nested. E.g. a VM Extension

Example

```
"vnetId1": "[resourceId('AE06-Mgmt-RG','Microsoft.Network/virtualNetworks', parameters('virtualNetworkName'))]",
"vnetId2": "[resourceId('Microsoft.Network/virtualNetworks', variables('virtualNetworkName'))]"
```

The above example shows two ways of using the resource ID helper function to determine the Id of a virtual network. First one uses the resource group, resource type, and resource name. The second example uses only the resource Type and resource name. The second example assumes the resource group to be same as the template being deployed to.

2. Resource Group – Resource Function

This helper function returns an object that represents the current resource group to which the template is being deployed.
The generic syntax to use this is:

```
resourceGroup()
```

No parameters are needed in this helper function.
Example

```
"vhdStorageName": "[concat('vhdstorage', uniqueString(resourceGroup().id))]",
"storageAccountResourceGroup": "[resourcegroup().name]",
"location": "[resourceGroup().location]"
```

The above example shows 3 uses of the resource group helper functions. First one uses the ID of the resource group, second uses the name property and third uses the location for the current resource group.

3. Subscription – Resource Function

The generic syntax to use this is:

```
subscription()
```

No parameters are needed in this helper function.
Example

```
"subscriptionId": "[subscription().subscriptionId]"
```

The above example is straightforward. It fetches the subscription Id of the current subscription.

4. Concat – String Function

This function is used to concatenate (i.e. combine) two or more values.
The generic syntax to use this is:

```
concat (array1, array2, array3, ...)
```

At least 1 array is needed for concat to work.

Example

```
"subnetRef": "[concat(variables('vNetId'), '/subnets/', variables('subnetName'))]"
```

The above example combines (or concatenates) 3 text values. First value is the value of variable vNetId. Second value is a string "/subnets/". Third value is the value of the variable subnet Name.

These are the most common Helper functions that you will use in 80%-90% of the templates.

To check the complete list of Helper Functions, check this official link: Azure Resource Manager template functions

CHAPTER 4 - BUILDING YOUR FIRST ARM TEMPLATE

First Steps to automating deployments

In this chapter, we will use the knowledge learned in previous chapters and will build a basic ARM template. To follow this chapter, you can use any text editor which can provide JSON syntax highlighting. We will be looking at using Visual Studio to author ARM templates in a future chapter. Visual Studio can provide JSON outlining and is a very powerful tool for authoring ARM templates.

Let us assume that you want to deploy a storage account and build a virtual network in Azure. You want to automate the process and need to repeat the process in various environments. ARM templates fit the bill for the solution of this problem.

In the next few sections, we will build each section of the template and then at the end will check the complete template.

1. Template Header

This section is very basic and contains just the schema and the content version. You can use the content version to manage the development versions of the template as you make changes to your templates in the future.

```
"$schema": "https://schema.management.azure.com/schemas/2015-01-01/deploymentTemplate.json#",
"contentVersion": "1.0.0.0",
```

2. Parameters

Here we define all the inputs we need from the end users. We provide default values for those parameters for which we know what the most common values will be based on our environment. For the current template we define two parameters:

- **vhdStorageName** – This is the name of the storage account in Azure which will be created by the deployment of this template.
- **virtualNetworkName** – This is the name of the Virtual Network which will be created by the deployment of this template.

As a best practice, provide the metadata, describing what each parameter is for. Also, note that we have used Pascal casing to name the parameters with very descriptive names.

```
"parameters": {
"vhdStorageName": {
"type": "string",
"minLength": 1,
"defaultValue": "mystorage101",
"metadata": {
"description": "Name of the Storage Account."
}
},
"virtualNetworkName": {
"type": "string",
"metadata": {
"description": "Name of the virtual network."
}
}
},
```

3. Variables

Next, we add some variables for the values which will be reused later in the template in the resources section. We create variables for all those reusable values for which we know what their value at deployment will be. We define 4 variables in this template:

- **addressPrefix** – Address prefix for the Virtual Network
- **subnetName** – Subnet name which will be created under the virtual network
- **subnetPrefix** – Subnet prefix for the subnet, which will be created under the virtual network
- **vhdStorageType** – Type of the storage account. Here we used Standard locally redundant storage (LRS)

Variables section look as below:

```
"variables": {
"addressPrefix": "10.0.0.0/16",
"subnetName": "Subnet",
"subnetPrefix": "10.0.0.0/24",
"vhdStorageType": "Standard_LRS"
},
```

4. Resources

Now comes the last and main section i.e. Resources. Here we define both the resources for our template:

- Storage Account
- Virtual Network

Let us look at each of these resources one by one.

A. Storage Account Resource

This resource has following properties (or key-value pairs):

1. **Type** – Type of the resource is set to Microsoft.Storage/storageAccounts. This is what tells the Azure that the current resource is a Storage Account
2. **Name** – This defines the name of the storage account to be deployed based on the parameter to the template
3. **API Version** – this is the standard version for the REST API in Azure
4. **Location** – This is the Azure location. The location is found dynamically based on the location of the resource group to which this template will be deployed.
5. **tags** – only one tag is defined for the display name. You should have more tags in case of a production-ready template
6. **properties** – This is where you tell Azure what kind of storage account you need. Here the account type is set using the value of the variable vhdStorageType.

B. Virtual Network Resource

This resource has below properties (or key-value pairs):

1. **Type** – Type of the resource is set to Microsoft.Network/virtualNetworks. This is what tells the Azure that the current resource is a Virtual Network
2. **Name** – This defines the name of the virtual network to be deployed based on the parameter to the template
3. **API Version** – this is the standard version for the REST API in Azure
4. **Location** – This is the Azure location. The location is found dynamically based on the location of the resource group to which this template will be deployed.
5. **tags** – only one tag is defined for the display name. You should have more tags in case of a production-ready template
6. **properties** – This is where you define the address space for the virtual network. You also define the subnet under the virtual network here.

The resources section look like below:

```
"resources": [
{
"type": "Microsoft.Storage/storageAccounts",
"name": "[parameters('vhdStorageName')]",
"apiVersion": "2015-06-15",
```

```json
"location": "[resourceGroup().location]",
"tags": {
"displayName": "StorageAccount"
},
"properties": {
"accountType": "[variables('vhdStorageType')]"
}
},
{
"apiVersion": "2015-06-15",
"type": "Microsoft.Network/virtualNetworks",
"name": "[parameters('virtualNetworkName')]",
"location": "[resourceGroup().location]",
"tags": {
"displayName": "VirtualNetwork"
},
"properties": {
"addressSpace": {
"addressPrefixes": [
"[variables('addressPrefix')]"
]
},
"subnets": [
{
"name": "[variables('subnetName')]",
"properties": {
"addressPrefix": "[variables('subnetPrefix')]"
}
}
]
}
}
]
```

Complete Template

Here is the complete template build from all the sections discussed above. You can copy and use this template for testing and working along with next deployment chapters.

```json
{
"$schema": "https://schema.management.azure.com/schemas/2015-01-01/deploymentTemplate.json#",
"contentVersion": "1.0.0.0",
"parameters": {
"vhdStorageName": {
"type": "string",
"minLength": 1,
"defaultValue": "mystorage101",
"metadata": {
```

```json
        "description": "Name of the Storage Account."
      }
    },
    "virtualNetworkName": {
      "type": "string",
      "metadata": {
        "description": "Name of the virtual network."
      }
    }
  },
  "variables": {
    "addressPrefix": "10.0.0.0/16",
    "subnetName": "Subnet",
    "subnetPrefix": "10.0.0.0/24",
    "vhdStorageType": "Standard_LRS"
  },
  "resources": [
    {
      "type": "Microsoft.Storage/storageAccounts",
      "name": "[parameters('vhdStorageName')]",
      "apiVersion": "2015-06-15",
      "location": "[resourceGroup().location]",
      "tags": {
        "displayName": "StorageAccount"
      },
      "properties": {
        "accountType": "[variables('vhdStorageType')]"
      }
    },
    {
      "apiVersion": "2015-06-15",
      "type": "Microsoft.Network/virtualNetworks",
      "name": "[parameters('virtualNetworkName')]",
      "location": "[resourceGroup().location]",
      "tags": {
        "displayName": "VirtualNetwork"
      },
      "properties": {
        "addressSpace": {
          "addressPrefixes": [
            "[variables('addressPrefix')]"
          ]
        },
        "subnets": [
          {
            "name": "[variables('subnetName')]",
            "properties": {
              "addressPrefix": "[variables('subnetPrefix')]"
            }
          }
```

```
        ]
      }
    }
  ]
}
```

In the next chapters, we will learn how to deploy this template.

CHAPTER 5 - DEPLOYING TEMPLATE USING AZURE PORTAL

GUI based deployment

Now that you have a fully functional ARM template we want to deploy this template to Azure. There are various options to deploy a template to Azure. Using Azure portal is by far the easiest and most intuitive option for the deployment.

Follow the steps in this chapter to deploy your template to Azure.

Pre-requisites

Things you should know before deployment

1. **Azure Subscription** – where you want to deploy your template
2. **Resource Group** – This is the resource group in Azure where you will be deploying your template. You can create a new resource group (for the resources that will be deployed by the template) or use an existing one.
3. **Parameters** – Value of the input parameters to the template should be known to you for the deployment. Follow all your naming conventions when defining the parameters for deployments of resources in Azure.

Steps for Deployment

1. First, log into the Azure Portal.
2. Next, go to "New" and type "Template deployment" in the search box and hit enter.

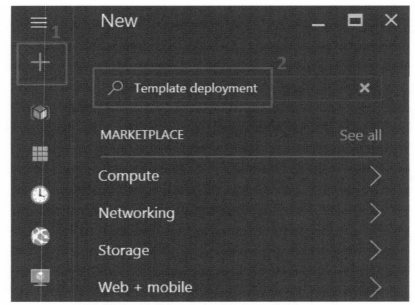

3. Next, click on the **Template Deployment** and then click on "Create"

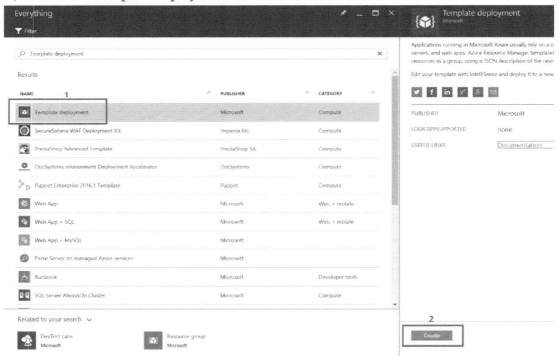

4. Now click on the "**Build your own template in the editor**". It will open a panel to paste your template.

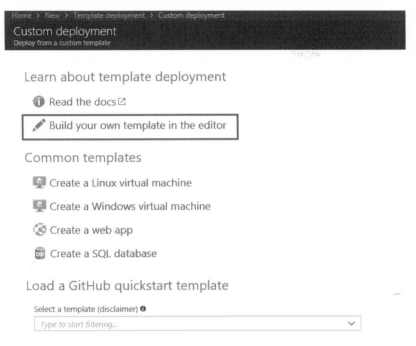

Custom deployment
Deploy from a custom template

Learn about template deployment

ⓘ Read the docs ↗

✏ Build your own template in the editor

Common templates

🖥 Create a Linux virtual machine

🖥 Create a Windows virtual machine

🌐 Create a web app

🗄 Create a SQL database

Load a GitHub quickstart template

Select a template (disclaimer) ⓘ

Type to start filtering...   ⌄

5. Delete whatever is auto-populated in the template area. Copy your whole json template and paste it here. Note that the left section in the new panel will update to show you what parameters, variables, and resources you have in the template. You can alternatively click on "Load file" and load your template from JSON file on the computer. Click on "Save" once done.

6. Next, you can
    1. Provide the Resource Group name and Location where you want to do the deployment.
    2. Click on the **"Edit Parameters"** at the top to provide parameters via json as well. We will discuss this in the upcoming chapter as well.
    3. You can also provide the parameter names manually. The parameters will be automatically picked from the template. The parameters for which the default value is provided in the template will be automatically populated. Rest you will have to provide the inputs.
    4. Select the checkbox to agree to the terms and conditions
    5. Click on "Purchase" to validate and deploy the template.

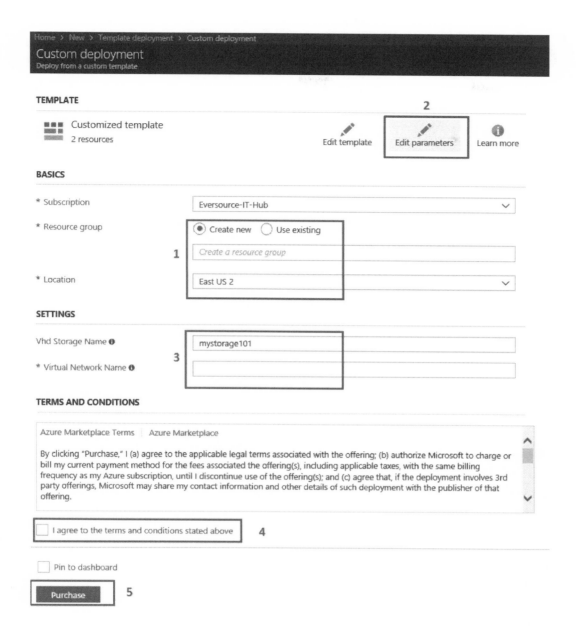

You can monitor the job performing the deployments and progress of the same. After some time the deployment will finish successfully and you can view the resources in the resource group you selected.

CHAPTER 6 - DEPLOYING TEMPLATE USING AZURE POWERSHELL

Command based automated deployment

Now we will look at **Azure PowerShell** as more programmatic and automated way to deploy the template.

Pre-requisites

Things you should know before deployment

1. **Azure PowerShell** – This should be installed on the machine from where the Steps will be followed. If you don't have this then use this link to get it: Get Azure PowerShell
2. **Azure Subscription** – where you want to deploy your template
3. **Resource Group** – This is the resource group in Azure where you will be deploying your template. You can create a new resource group (for the resources that will be deployed by the template) or use an existing one.
4. **Parameters** – Value of the input parameters to the template should be known to you for the deployment. Follow all your naming conventions when defining the parameters for deployments of resources in Azure.
5. **Internet Connectivity** – This should be present on the machine from where the Steps will be followed for connectivity to Azure

Steps for Deployment

- First, launch a PowerShell window as an Administrator
- Then, log into the Azure account.

Run the below cmdlet to log into Azure:

```
Add-AzureRmAccount
```

- Select appropriate Azure Subscription

You have two choices here. You can either use below cmdlet to use Subscription ID

```
Set-AzureRmContext -SubscriptionID <YourSubscriptionId>
```

Or you can use the Subscription name with the below cmdlet:

```
Select-AzureRmSubscription -SubscriptionName "<Your Subscription Name>"
```

- Next, if you already have a resource group to which you want to deploy the template then skip this step. Else create a new resource group. A resource in Azure ARM architecture can only exist in a resource group.

Use below cmdlet to create a new Resource Group:

```
New-AzureRmResourceGroup -Name TestResourceGroup01 -Location "Central US"
```

- Before deploying the Resource Template to Azure, you should Test it. This step is optional but highly recommended.

Use the below cmdlet to test and **validate** your template:

```
Test-AzureRmResourceGroupDeployment -ResourceGroupName TestResourceGroup01 -TemplateFile <PathToJsonTemplate>
```

- Now comes the last step i.e. to deploy the template. You have two options when deploying the template. You can either deploy a template without any parameters (if none are required) or you need to specify the parameters. Let's check both these options next.

Deploying Template which doesn't need Parameters

You can deploy such template using New-AzureRmResourceGroupDeployment cmdlet. If the template file is on a local directory then use the below cmdlet:

```
New-AzureRmResourceGroupDeployment -Name ExampleDeployment -ResourceGroupName TestResourceGroup01 -TemplateFile <PathToTemplate>
```

If the template file is uploaded to some hosted location and is accessible via a link, then use the below cmdlet to deploy the template:

```
New-AzureRmResourceGroupDeployment -Name ExampleDeployment -ResourceGroupName TestResourceGroup01 -Templat
eUri <LinkToTemplate>
```

Deploying Template with Parameters

Deploying of the template is exactly similar to the previous section. You use the same cmdlet. To specify the parameter, you have 4 options. Use the below cmdlets for the option you want to use.

Option 1 – Using Inline Parameter

```
New-AzureRmResourceGroupDeployment -Name ExampleDeployment -ResourceGroupName TestResourceGroup01 -Templat
eFile <PathToTemplate> -myParameterName "parameterValue" -secondParameterName "secondParameterValue"
```

Option 2 – Using Parameter Object

```
$parameters = @{"<ParameterName>"="<Parameter Value>"}
New-AzureRmResourceGroupDeployment -Name ExampleDeployment -ResourceGroupName TestResourceGroup01 -Templat
eFile <PathToTemplate> -TemplateParameterObject $parameters
```

Option 3 – Using Parameter file which is in local environment

```
New-AzureRmResourceGroupDeployment -Name ExampleDeployment -ResourceGroupName TestResourceGroup01 -Templat
eFile <PathToTemplate> -TemplateParameterFile <PathToParameterFile>
```

Option 4 – Using Parameter file which is located externally and can be referenced via Link

```
New-AzureRmResourceGroupDeployment -Name ExampleDeployment -ResourceGroupName TestResourceGroup01 -Templat
eUri <LinkToTemplate> -TemplateParameterUri <LinkToParameterFile>
```

Key Gotchas

1. If you provide values for a parameter in both the local parameter file and inline, the inline value takes precedence.
2. You cannot use inline parameters with an external parameter file. All inline parameters are ignored when you specify "TemplateParameterUri" parameter.
3. As a best practice, do not store sensitive information in the parameters file e.g. Local admin password. Instead of this, either provide these dynamically using inline parameters, or store them using the Azure Key vault and then reference the key vault in your parameters file.

CHAPTER 7 - CREATING PARAMETERS FILE FOR AN ARM TEMPLATE

Providing inputs to your template

Y ou can pass the input values for the Parameters in your ARM template using an additional JSON file. This additional file is what we will be referring to as Parameters File. The only restriction on a parameters file is that the size of the parameter file cannot be more than 64 KB. Parameters file follows a similar structure to the ARM Template. They are very simple as compared to the ARM template.

In all they have 3 sections as explained below:

1. **$schema** – Required Object – Location of the JSON schema file that describes the version of the template language.
2. **contentVersion** – Required Object – Version of the template (such as 1.2.0.20). When deploying resources using the template, this value can be used to make sure that the right template is being used.
3. **parameters** – Required Object – This is a JSON object which contains various objects as it's members. Each object within the "parameters" object represent a value for a parameter corresponding to your ARM template.

Let's check how the parameters file will look like for the ARM template we have built earlier for deploying Storage Account and a Virtual Network.

```
{
"$schema": "https://schema.management.azure.com/schemas/2015-01-01/deploymentParameters.json#",
"contentVersion": "1.0.0.0",
"parameters": {
"vhdStorageName": {
"value": "harvestingstorage101"
```

```
},
"virtualNetworkName": {
"value": "testvNet101"
}
}
}
```

Note that the only 2 parameter values are provided. These correspond to the parameters in the ARM template.
Note: The parameter names should match to the parameters defined in the ARM template.

CHAPTER 8 - AUTHORING ARM TEMPLATES USING VISUAL STUDIO

Leveraging Visual Studio for all development

Visual Studio is a very powerful tool when it comes to authoring ARM Templates. It is very feature rich for not just authoring but also for validating and performing the deployments.

Key features which make it a tool of our choice are:

- In-house support for ARM Templates
- Smart IntelliSense
- Pre-populated templates for various Azure resources
- JSON Outlining
- Easy Deployment options

The screenshots in this chapter are from Visual Studio 2013. You can use other newer versions as well.

Pre-Requisites

You need to have Azure SDK installed to get true power of Visual Studio with Azure integration. If you don't have it already, you can install the same from here: Azure SDK Downloads

Authoring First ARM Template in Visual Studio

Authoring with Visual Studio is very easy.

1. To get started just launch the Visual Studio from the Start menu.
2. Next, Create a new Project of type "Azure Resource Group" by navigating to Templates -> Visual C# -> Cloud

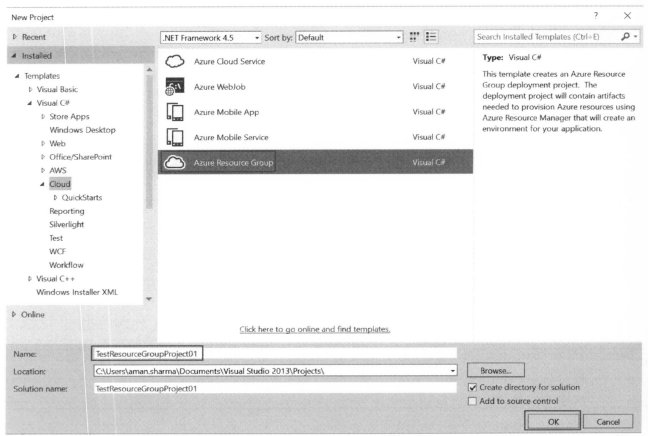

3. Next, you will be presented with a dialog to "Select Azure Template". If you want to author from scratch then choose a Blank Template. Else select one of the starter templates. For this chapter, we will be using "Windows Virtual Machine" Template.

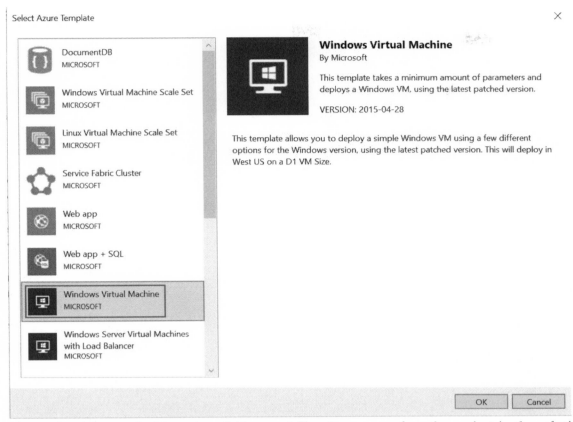

4. The project is created with various folders and files. You can explore the project in the solution explorer in Visual Studio.

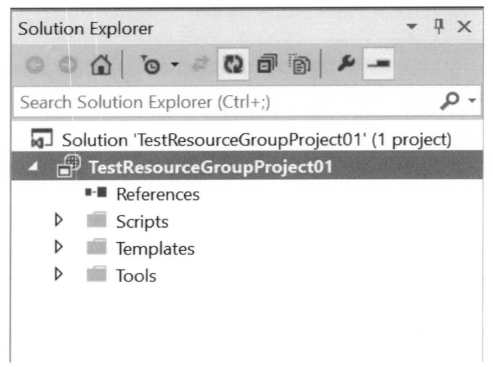

Let us see what these folders and files are:

    a. **Scripts**: The single PS1 file is to create a new Resource Group and deploy the ARM Template. It use "New–AzureRmResourceGroupDeployment" PowerShell cmdlet to deploy the template.

    b. **Templates**: "WindowsVirtualMachine.json" is the main ARM Template file that we are interested in Also, "WindowsVirtualMachine.parameters.json" is the parameters file for the ARM template.

    c. **Tools**: This folder contains the "AzCopy.exe" file to help you copy any artifacts to Azure.

5. Double click and open the "WindowsVirtualMachine.json" file to open it. You will be presented with a hug JSON file. Collapse the section by clicking the small "-" signs to the left of the file. Also, notice the **JSON Outline** panel to the left. This is your biggest friend in Visual Studio when authoring ARM Templates

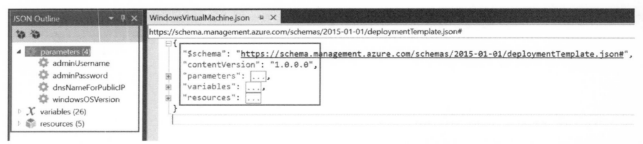

You can immediately notice that key sections both in the template in the middle and in the JSON Outline panel on the left (in the image above) are:

    a. parameters

    b. variables

    c. resources

You can click on any of the elements in the left JSON Outline panel and the same section will be highlighted in the center, in the JSON template file.

6. Next, let us look at JSON Outline panel and check how it can provide us more information and help us in authoring templates.

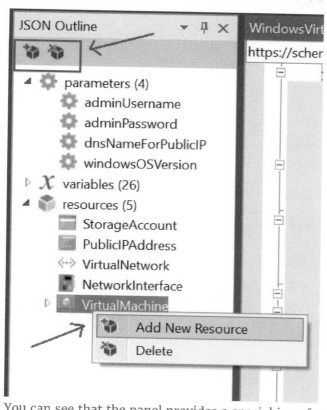

You can see that the panel provides a special icon for each type of the resource. In our current template the various resources listed are:

a. StorageAccount
b. PublicIPAddress
c. VirtualNetwork
d. NetworkInterface
e. VirtualMachine

Click on each of the resources and inspect how their JSON structure looks and differs. You will immediately notice that the major difference in each of these resources is in their **Type** and **Properties**.

Adding New Resource

Let's assume you want to add a new resource to this template. You have 2 ways to achieve the same:

6. **Method 1** – Create a new resource by modifying and adding the JSON for the new resource in the template.

7. **Method 2** – Let Visual Studio add the resource for you. Right-click anywhere in the resources area of the JSON Outline Panel or the small "+" box at the top left of the panel (as shown in the image above) and VS will give you a new popup to add the resource from pre-defined resources as shown below.

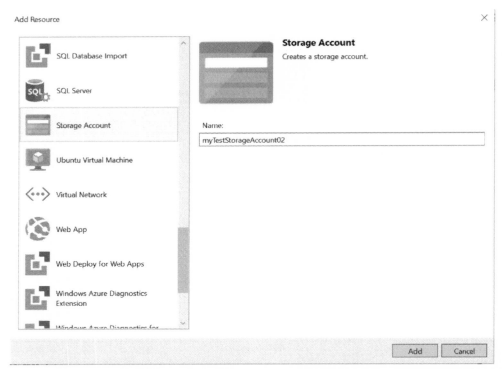

Once you click Add the JSON for the resource will be added to the template and the corresponding new element will appear in the JSON Outline Panel.

Deleting a Resource

If you need to delete a resource, simply right-click on that resource in the JSON outline panel on the left and then select "Delete Resource".

Using Intellisense

The last thing to notice is the use of **Intellisense** in Visual Studio which helps you as you are editing th templates.

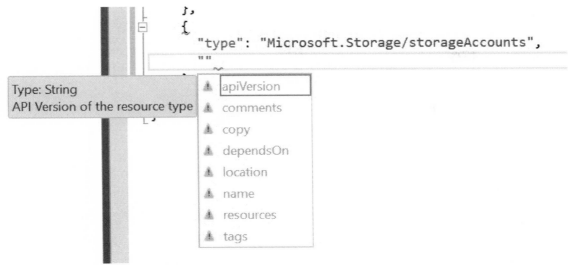

When you type quotes the closing quotes are automatically provided. Also, as you can see in the above image the various valid values, that can come there are also shown along with small tooltip about the data type. If the Intellisense doesn't come up automatically, then press Ctrl + Space to get Intellisense.

In the end, the Visual Studio makes authoring ARM templates much more manageable and easy for you.

CHAPTER 9 - DEPLOYING ARM TEMPLATES USING VISUAL STUDIO

Deploying right from the authoring tool

n this chapter we will see how to use Visual Studio (VS) to deploy the template without leaving VS. Deploying with Visual Studio is very simple, straightforward and very intuitive.

Just follow the below steps.

1. Either go to the Solution Explorer -> Right Click on the project and select "Deploy -> New Deployment" as shown below:

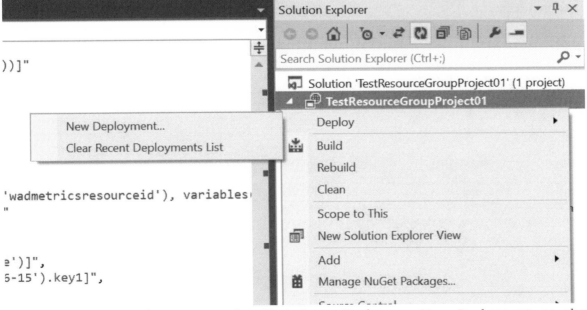

Or you can go to the menu option Project -> Deploy -> New Deployment as shown below:

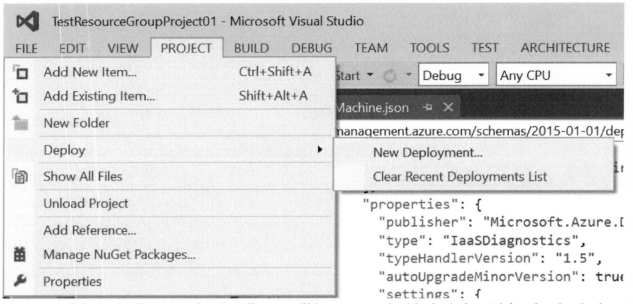

Once you click on the "New Deployment", you will be presented with the below Dialog for the deployment

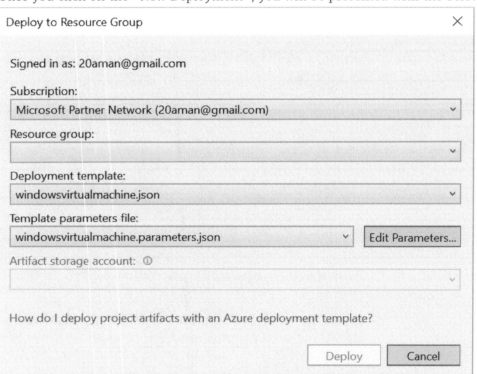

If you are not logged in then it will ask you to log into your Azure account.

2. In the Dialog for "Deploy to Resource Group" select the Subscription by clicking on the first drop down.

3. Next click on the drop down for the Resource Group. You can either select an existing Resource Group or you can click on "<Create New...>" option to create a new resource group for the current deployment.

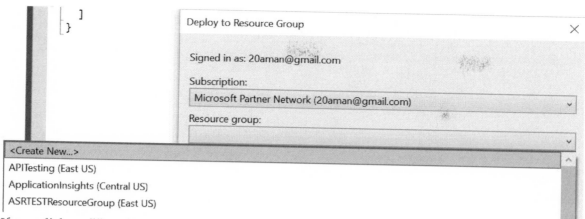

]
}

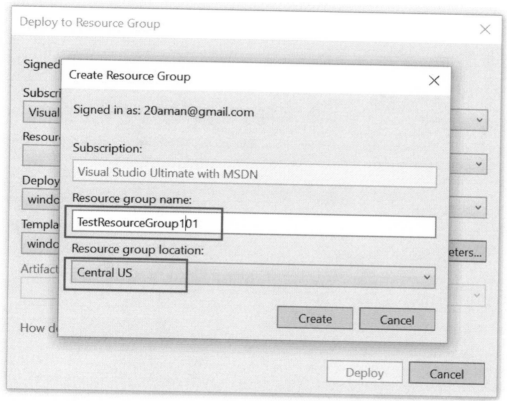

<Create New...>
APITesting (East US)
ApplicationInsights (Central US)
ASRTESTResourceGroup (East US)

If you click on "" option to create a new Resource Group then you will be presented with an additional popup.

In this additional popup, type the name for your new resource group and the location in Azure where this should be created. Click "Create" once done in the additional popup.

4. Next, we are going to provide the value for the parameters. Go ahead and click on the "Edit Parameters..." link in the "Deploy to Resource Group" dialog. This will open another popup to provide the parameters. Button to edit parameters is shown below:

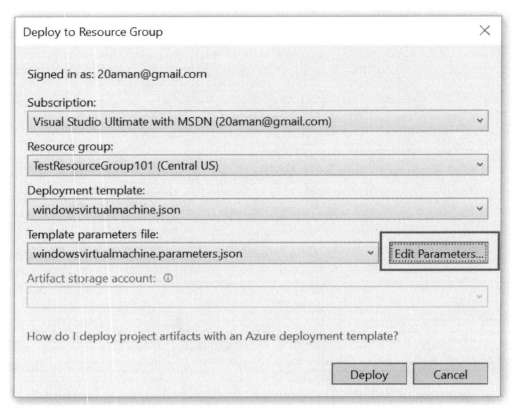

Additional dialog to provide parameters is shown below:

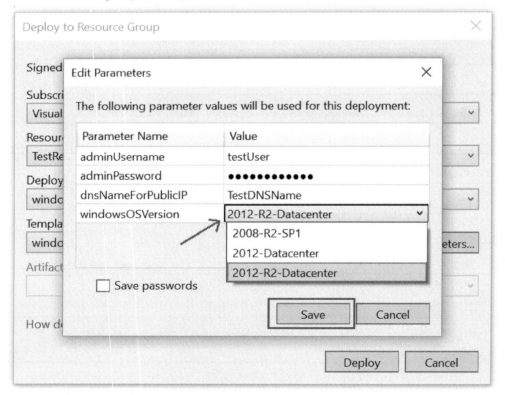

Note the following points in the parameters:

a. Corresponding to the string parameters, a text box is provided.
b. For the secure string parameters like password, a secure password text box is provided.
c. Corresponding to the parameters for which you have defined the "Allowed Values" in your template, a combo box (or drop Down) is provided with the "default Value" selected by default.

Click Ok once done

5. Next, click on the Deploy button to deploy the template to Azure.
6. You can check the results in the **Outputs** window in the Visual Studio. Along with time stamp, it will show you what steps Visual Studio took to perform the deployment. It uses the values of parameters you provided and uses the PowerShell script to deploy the resources. You will notice the PowerShell window opening and prompt for the Admin Password.

Note 1: The PowerShell window may not come above as active window. Just search and click on the window in your Taskbar.

Provide the password and hit Enter as shown below:

```
C:\Windows\System32\WindowsPowerShell\v1.0\powershell.exe

cmdlet New-AzureRmResourceGroupDeployment at command pipeline position 1
Supply values for the following parameters:
(Type !? for Help.)
adminPassword: ********
```

Note 2: It may take some time to complete the deployment after that. Wait and do not close the PowerShell window. It should automatically close once done.

Note 3: Once the deployment completes the last line in the Output window in Visual Studio will be: "Successfully deployed template..." as shown below:

```
Output

Show output from: TestResourceGroup101

17:22:48 -                          Microsoft.Azure.Commands.ResourceManager.Cmdlets.SdkModels.DeploymentVariable],
17:22:48 -                          [dnsNameForPublicIP,
17:22:48 -                          Microsoft.Azure.Commands.ResourceManager.Cmdlets.SdkModels.DeploymentVariable],
17:22:48 -                          [windowsOSVersion,
17:22:48 -                          Microsoft.Azure.Commands.ResourceManager.Cmdlets.SdkModels.DeploymentVariable]}
17:22:48 - ParametersString    :
17:22:48 -
17:22:48 -                          Name              Type                          Value
17:22:48 -                          ===============   ==========================    ==========
17:22:48 -                          adminUsername     String                        testUser
17:22:48 -                          adminPassword     SecureString
17:22:48 -                          dnsNameForPublicIP String                       TestDNSName
17:22:48 -                          windowsOSVersion  String                        2012-R2-Datacenter
17:22:48 -
17:22:48 - Outputs              :
17:22:48 - OutputsString        :
17:22:48 -
17:22:48 -
17:22:48 -
17:22:48 - Successfully deployed template 'c:\users\aman.sharma\documents\visual studio 2013\projects\testresourcegrou

Error List   Output   Azure App Service Activity
```

This is it! Navigate to the Azure portal and validate the deployed resources in your selected resource group.

CHAPTER 10 - ITERATING AND CREATING MULTIPLE INSTANCES OF A RESOURCE

Writing less and doing more

n Azure Resource Manager (ARM) templates, you can define the variable once and then iterate/loop over that definition and create multiple instances of that resource. There are 3 special constructs in ARM templates to help you with this.

These **constructs** are:

- **copy** – This is a property that is defined within the resource. This is the construct which when defined indicates that this resource needs to be looped over and created multiple times. It also specifies the number of times to iterate via "count" property.
- **copyIndex()** – Used to access the current iteration value. Its value for the first iteration is **zero**. For the second iteration, its value is 1 and so on... You can pass it an integer (number) as a parameter. Whatever number you pass that will become the value for the first iteration and subsequent iterations. E.g. copyIndex(20) will compute to 20 in the first iteration, 21 in the second iteration and so on.
- **length** – This is the method of arrays. It computes the number of elements in an array. It can be used to set the "count" property of "copy" construct.

Note: Arrays are always **zero indexed**. What that means is that the first element of the array is indexed at 0, the second element of the array is indexed at 1, and so on...

1. Simple Example

Let us understand these constructs using an example.

```
"parameters": {
"count": {
"type": "int",
"defaultValue": 3
}
},
"resources": [
{
"name": "[concat('HarvestingClouds-', copyIndex(100))]",
"type": "Microsoft.Web/sites",
"location": "Central US",
"apiVersion": "2015-08-01",
"copy": {
"name": "websitescopy",
"count": "[parameters('count')]"
},
"properties": {
"serverFarmId": "hostingPlanName"
}
}
]
```

The above example will **result** in creation of below 3 web apps in Azure:

- HarvestingClouds-100
- HarvestingClouds-101
- HarvestingClouds-102

Note the usage of "copy" property in the above code example:

```
"copy": {
"name": "websitescopy",
"count": "[parameters('count')]"
}
```

As you can notice above, the value of this property is another JSON object. This object has further tw
properties:

- First is the name property, which provides the name to the looping construct. This can be any meaningfu
  name.
- The second property is the count, which specifies how many times this resource definition should b
  deployed. Note that the value is set to the parameter named "count". The name of the parameter can b
  anything but the value of the parameter has to be a number (i.e. an integer).

Next, note how the name of the web application is constructed using the copyIndex() helper function.

```
"name": "[concat('HarvestingClouds-', copyIndex(100))]"
```

The above value uses two helper functions. First is the "concat()" which is concatenating (i.e. joining) two values. The first value is the prefix string "HarvestingClouds-". Second parameter and the second helper function is copyIndex(100). This specifies the current iteration value, which is offset with 100. So for the first iteration, the value will be 0+100 = 100, for the second iteration the value will be 1+100 = 101 and so on...

2. Example with an Array

Let's assume that you want to deploy multiple web apps for different purposes. You need one web app for production, one for Staging or testing and one for Development. You want to name the web apps deployed with the purpose concatenated. The below example uses an array to set the values for the web app name:

```
"parameters": {
"purpose": {
"type": "array",
"defaultValue": [
"Production",
"Staging",
"Development"
]
}
},
"resources": [
{
"name": "[concat('HarvestingClouds-', parameters('purpose')[copyIndex()])]",
"type": "Microsoft.Web/sites",
"location": "Central US",
"apiVersion": "2015-08-01",
"copy": {
"name": "websitescopy",
"count": "[length(parameters('purpose'))]"
},
"properties": {
"serverFarmId": "hostingPlanName"
}
}
]
```

The **output** of the above sample will be 3 web apps deployed in Azure with following names:

- HarvestingClouds-Production
- HarvestingClouds-Staging
- HarvestingClouds-Development

Note in the above code sample that the parameter "purpose" is an array of 3 values i.e. Production, Staging, and Development. Then in the "copy" construct the count property is set using the length of this array as shown below. As there are 3 elements in the array, the value of count will be 3 and the resource will be deployed 3 times.

```
"count": "[length(parameters('purpose'))]"
```

Next, the name of the web app is set using the copyIndex() and the array itself as shown below:

```
"name": "[concat('HarvestingClouds-', parameters('purpose')[copyIndex()])]"
```

As earlier, it uses a concat helper function to add two strings. The first string is simple text i.e. "HarvestingClouds-", which becomes the prefix for the web app name. Second is finding out the value of the array based on the current iteration. For the first iteration, copyIndex() will compute to zero, therefore the second parameter becomes parameters('purpose')[0]. This will fetch the 0th element of the array which is Production. Similarly, for the second iteration, copyIndex() will compute to 1, therefore the second parameter becomes parameters('purpose')[1]. This will fetch the second element of the array (or element at index value 1) which is Staging, and so on...

3. Depending upon resources being deployed by the copy Loop

Let's assume you want to deploy a storage account. But you want to deploy it only after all the web apps are deployed by the loop. In this scenario, the dependsOn property of a resource is set to the name of the "copy" property of the resource, rather than the resource itself.

```
{
"apiVersion": "2015-06-15",
"type": "Microsoft.Storage/storageAccounts",
"name": "teststorage101",
"location": "[resourceGroup().location]",
"properties": {
"accountType": "Standard_LRS"
}
"dependsOn": ["websitescopy"]
}
```

Note above that the dependsOn property is set to the name property of the copy in the earlier web app example. This storage account will not be deployed until all 3 web apps are not deployed.

4. Limitations

There are two limitations on the use of the copy to iterate and create multiple resource instances:

1. **Nested Resources** – You cannot use a copy loop for a nested resource. If you need to create multiple instances of a resource that you typically define as nested within another resource, you must instead create the resource as a top-level resource and define the relationship with the parent resource through the **type** and **name** properties.
2. **Looping Properties of a Resource** – You can only use copy on resource types, not on properties within a resource type. E.g. Creating multiple data disks within a VM.

That is all there is to iterate and creating multiple resources from a single definition. When your templates will start becoming complex then these constructs/helper functions will help you a lot. E.g. you may need to deploy multiple load balanced resources, then you can use the concepts defined in this chapter.

CHAPTER 11 - VISUALIZING ARM TEMPLATES AND GENERATING DIAGRAMS

Easy visualizations

When developing ARM Templates, from time to time you will need to:

- Visualize your ARM Templates
- Generate Diagrams for your ARM Templates

Microsoft has provided an Open Source tool for this named "ARMVIZ" (short for ARM Visualizer). This tool can be accessed by navigating to the below URL:

http://armviz.io/

Navigating ARMVIZ

ARMVIZ is a nice in-browser application to visualize all the components in a template. It also shows the dependencies between various components. Using this web application you can:

- Either visualize your own developed template,
- Or inspect existing templates on GitHub

Let's take a quick tour of the interface:

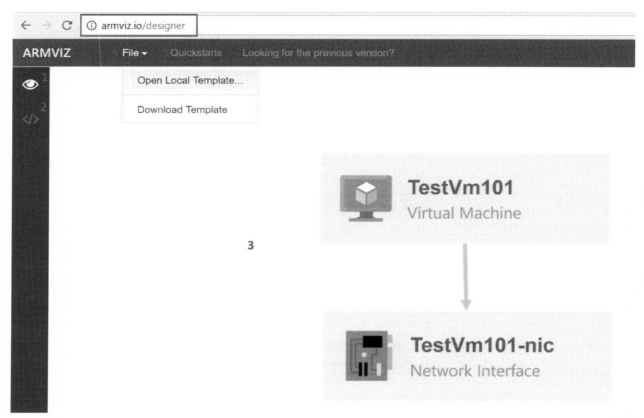

I have numbered various elements of the interface in the above diagram. Let's quickly review these elements:

1. **Designer** – This is represented by an "eye" icon on the left bar. This should be selected by default. If you are in the editor mode then you can click this and the diagram will be shown in the middle portion of the screen.
2. **Editor** – This is represented by "</>" text for code on the left bar. Clicking on this will take you to the editor portion of the ARMVIZ tool. In this area, you can edit your template while still in the tool. You can add or remove components. You can even edit the components or add dependencies.
3. **Canvas area** – This is the main screen (the middle area) where the template is displayed.
4. **File Menu** – This is the main and simple menu in the whole web application in the top bar. It has two options:
    a. **Open Local Template** – You can open an ARM Template JSON from your local computer to visualize using this menu option.
    b. **Download Template** – You can download the current template by using this menu option.
5. **Quickstart ARM Templates** – This is the link to an external library of Quickstart ARM Templates on GitHub. These starter templates can help you save a lot of time. Instead of starting from scratch you can use these templates to fasten the ARM Templates Development.

This is how the Editor portion of the tool looks like. Use this area to edit or update your template. **Note:** If there will be mistakes, such as missing parenthesis in your template, the designer will not show any diagram.

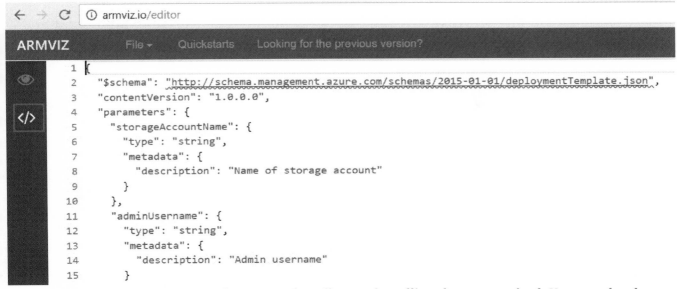

```
1  {
2    "$schema": "http://schema.management.azure.com/schemas/2015-01-01/deploymentTemplate.json",
3    "contentVersion": "1.0.0.0",
4    "parameters": {
5      "storageAccountName": {
6        "type": "string",
7        "metadata": {
8          "description": "Name of storage account"
9        }
10     },
11     "adminUsername": {
12       "type": "string",
13       "metadata": {
14         "description": "Admin username"
15       }
```

You can zoom into and zoom out of your template diagram by rolling the mouse wheel. You can also drag and position various elements. Take a screenshot once you have repositioned the elements as per your requirements and have zoomed to an appropriate level.

Below screenshot is taken from a much more complex template.

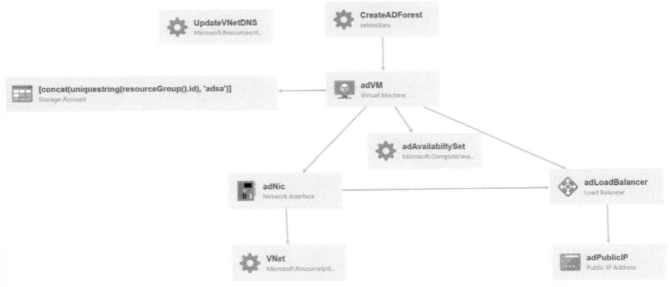

In conclusion, ARMVIZ can enable you to easily visualize your ARM Templates. It can empower you to generate diagrams for your documentation and to present to your team.

CHAPTER 12 - USING KEY VAULT TO SECURELY PROVIDE INFORMATION IN ARM TEMPLATES

Securing ARM Templates

W hen providing passwords and other secure and confidential information in ARM Templates, you need to ensure that you don't hardcode these values anywhere. You don't need to compromise the security of the system while trying to automate deployments. Your end goal is to try to automate as much as possible and reduce manual involvement.

Key Vaults are there to solve this problem without compromising any security. In fact, they make the whole solution more secure with least manual intervention.

Setting up the Key Vault

We first need to setup the Key Vault in Azure to be able to use it via ARM Template parameters.

1. **Create a Key Vault in Azure** by going to *New -> Security + Identity -> Key Vault*. Provide a name, subscription, resource group etc. and provision the Key Vault. Once it is created navigate to it by clicking on "More Services" and searching for Key Vault. Click on the name of the vault you created. E.g. In this example, we have named the key vault to "TestKeyVault101".

2. Next, we need to **Add a Secret** in the key vault. Click on the Secrets and then the + Add button at the top, as shown below:

Next, in the "Create a secret" blade, set the Upload Options to Manual. Provide a name and value to the secret. Value is the password you want to securely save. Ensure that the Enabled is set to Yes. Optionally you can set the activation and expiration dates. In this example, we are setting the Secret Name to "DefaultAdminPasswordSecret".

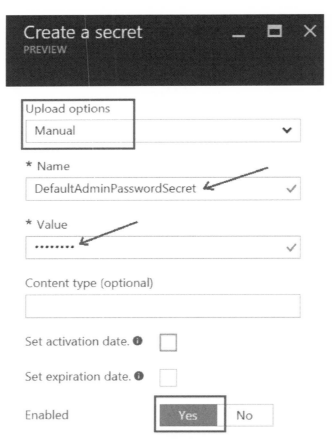

3. Next, we will set the **Access Policies** to provide access to the user under the context of which the templat will be deployed. This is the user which will be accessing the Key Vault. Go to Key Vault settings and selec

Access   Policies.   Add   the   new   user   as   shown   below:

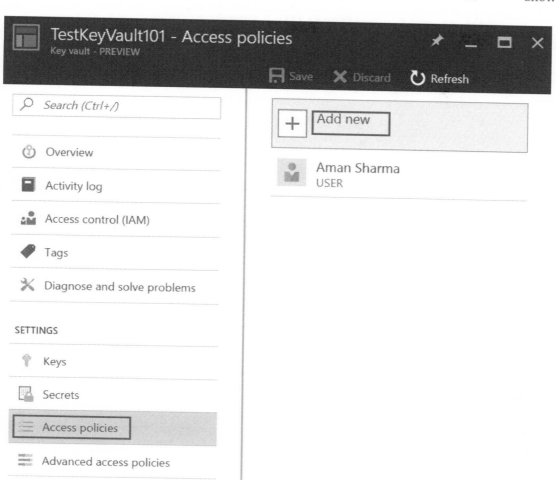

4. Next, we will set the **Advanced Access Policies** to indicate that this key vault can be accessed via ARM Templates. Go to Key Vault settings and select Advanced Access Policies. Ensure that the checkbox for *"Enable access to Azure Resource Manager for template deployment"* is checked as shown below:

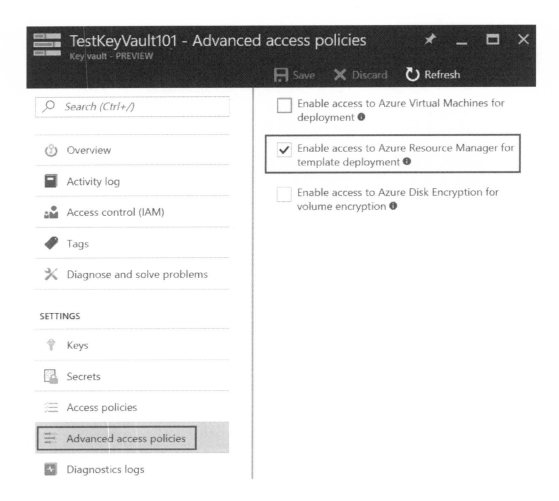

We are now all set with our Key Vault. Next, we will be using the secret we created to set the local Administrator user's password.

Using the Key Vault Secret in ARM Template

Let us assume that you have a JSON ARM Template which deploys a VM. One of the parameters in this template is AdminPassword. You want to use the Key Vault Secret to provide the value for this parameter.

First, ensure that the parameter is declared as *securestring* as shown below:

```
"adminPassword": {
"type": "securestring",
"metadata": {
"description": "Password for local admin account."
}
}
```

Next, we need to use the parameters file for this template. If you don't have one already create a new one. We can provide the reference to the Key Vault Secret as the value of admin user's password parameter in this file. General Syntax of providing reference is as shown follow:

```
"adminPassword": {
"reference": {
"keyVault": {
"id": "Key Vault Id Here"
},
"secretName": "Name of the secret in Azure Key Vault"
}
}
```

Now the ID in the above Syntax can be provided as:

/subscriptions/{guid}/resourceGroups/{group-name}/providers/Microsoft.KeyVault/vaults/{vault-name}.

Note to replace the *{guid}* with actual GUID for the subscription (without the curly braces), replace *{group-name}* with the actual name of the resource group and *{vault-name}* with the actual name of the Key Vault.

You can also find the Resource ID for the Key Vault by navigating to it in the Azure Portal and then checking it's properties as shown below:

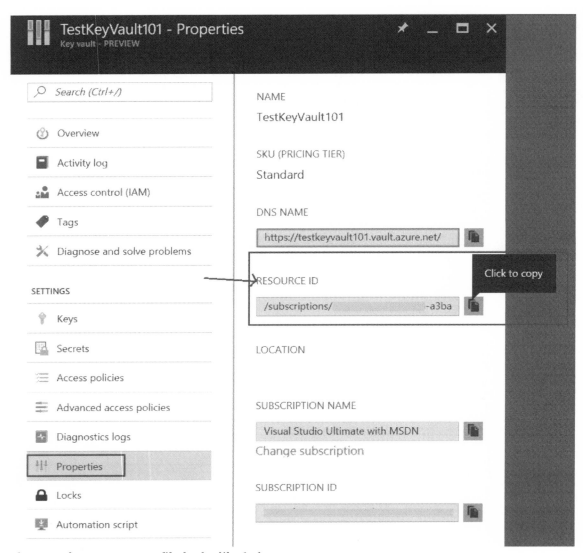

The complete parameter file looks like below:

```
{
"$schema": "http://schema.management.azure.com/schemas/2015-01-01/deploymentParameters.json#",
"contentVersion": "1.0.0.0",
"parameters": {
"OtherParameter": {
"value": "otherValue"
},
"adminPassword": {
"reference": {
"keyVault": {
"id": "/subscriptions/11111aaa-1a11-1a11-a1aa-1a1111a111a1/resourceGroups/TestRG101/providers/Microsoft.KeyVault/vaults/Te
tKeyVault101"
},
"secretName": "DefaultAdminPasswordSecret"
}
```

```
        }
    }
}
```

Next, deploy the template using PowerShell and pass this parameters file as explained here: Deploying Template Using Azure PowerShell.

Example PowerShell cmdlet to deploy will look like:

```
New-AzureRmResourceGroupDeployment –Name ExampleDeployment –ResourceGroupName TestResourceGroup01 –TemplateFile .\TemplateFile.json –TemplateParameterFile .\ParametersFile.json
```

Now that you know how to use values from Key Vaults, you can make the automated deployment of resources more secure in your environment.

CHAPTER 13 - PROVIDING POWERSHELL SCRIPTS TO RUN AFTER VM DEPLOYMENT VIA ARM TEMPLATE

Adding additional automation to deployment

By providing PowerShell Scripts to Run after VM deployment via ARM Template, you can accomplish various activities.

- You can setup different features and roles on the VM.
- You can setup a web server.
- You can setup SQL Database and configure it.
- You can configure custom policies
- And so on...

You first need to have PowerShell script files uploaded to a storage account. To do this you add an **Extension** source(*Microsoft.Compute/virtualMachines/extensions*) nested inside a VM. This extension resource should be of ype "**CustomScriptExtension**". You provide the URLs to the PowerShell scripts inside this custom script extension.

Preparation

As part of the preparation process you need to:

- Ensure that the PowerShell scripts are uploaded to the Storage Account and that you have the complete URL to the blob.
- Or you can upload the scripts to the GitHub and get the Raw file URL

- If there are more than one scripts then there should be one master script amongst all ps1 files which w.
internally invoke other files. This master file will be triggered via the template. Information of all file URI
will also be provided via the Template

Providing and configuring Scripts to Run After VM Deployment

Define the below resource to provide PowerShell scripts to be run after VM deployment:

```
{
"type": "Microsoft.Compute/virtualMachines/extensions",
"name": "MyCustomScriptExtension",
"apiVersion": "2015-05-01-preview",
"location": "[parameters('location')]",
"dependsOn": [
"[concat('Microsoft.Compute/virtualMachines/',parameters('vmName'))]"
],
"properties": {
"publisher": "Microsoft.Compute",
"type": "CustomScriptExtension",
"typeHandlerVersion": "1.7",
"autoUpgradeMinorVersion":true,
"settings": {
"fileUris": [
"http://Yourstorageaccount.blob.core.windows.net/customscriptfiles/start.ps1",
"http://Yourstorageaccount.blob.core.windows.net/customscriptfiles/secondaryScript.ps1",

],
"commandToExecute": "powershell.exe –ExecutionPolicy Unrestricted -File start.ps1"
}
}
}
```

How it works:

- Both the files i.e. start.ps1 and secondaryScript.ps1 are picked up from the storage account after VP
deployment. Ensure to replace the URLs with your actual storage account blob URLs. You can add more file
if needed.
- The "start.ps1" is the main PowerShell script which should be invoking the secondaryScript.ps1 internally
- CommandToExecutre property is used to invoke the start.ps1 PowerShell script on the deployed VM

Passing Parameters to the PowerShell Script dynamically

To pass the parameters to the PowerShell script use commandToExecute property.
One such example to pass the parameters is shown below:

```
"commandToExecute": "[concat('powershell.exe –ExecutionPolicy Unrestricted –File start.ps1', ' –domainName ', parameters
'domainNameParameter')]"
```

Note the use of "concat" helper function to create the value of the "commandToExecute". Also note that there is starting and trailing space in the second argument of the concat i.e. " –domainName ".

The parameter "domainNameParameter" should already be defined in the template in the parameters section. If the value of parameter "domainNameParameter" is "testdomain.com" then the dynamically generated command will become:

```
powershell.exe –ExecutionPolicy Unrestricted –File start.ps1 –domainName testdomain.com
```

Securing the Access to the PowerShell Script File in Storage account

Let us assume you want to deploy Windows VM with Protected settings. Then use the below sample to provide the PowerShell files.

```
{
"publisher": "Microsoft.Compute",
"type": "CustomScriptExtension",
"typeHandlerVersion": "1.7",
"settings": {
"fileUris": [
"http: //Yourstorageaccount.blob.core.windows.net/customscriptfiles/start.ps1"
]
},
"protectedSettings": {
"commandToExecute": "powershell.exe –ExecutionPolicy Unrestricted –start.ps1",
"storageAccountName": "yourStorageAccountName",
"storageAccountKey": "yourStorageAccountKey"
}
}
```

Note the use of "protectedSettings" above. This time you also specify the Storage Account Name and the Storage Account Key.

CHAPTER 14 - DEPLOYING A WINDOWS VM WITH OMS INTEGRATION VIA ARM TEMPLATES

Monitoring the Deployed VMs

You can deploy a Windows VM with OMS integration. You can have the OMS extension installed. And then you can onboard the VM to a specified workspace.

Prerequisites

You need already have an OMS workspace setup in your subscription. You need to have the following information about this OMS Workspace:

1. OMS workspace ID
2. OMS workspace Key

You may obtain the workspace ID and key by going to the Connected Sources tab in the Settings page in the OMS portal or to the Direct Agent blade in the Azure portal.

In the Azure Portal go to the Log Analytics -> Click on the OMS Workspace you want to use. Click on the "OMS portal" to navigate to the OMS Portal.

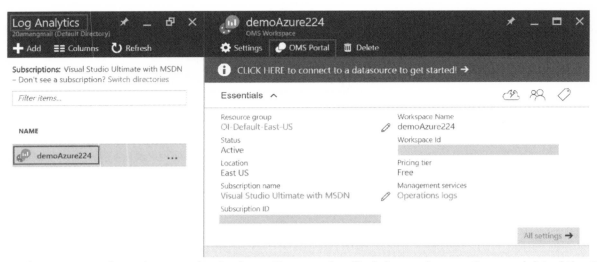

In the OMS portal, navigate to the Settings. You can also find the settings at the top right of the OMS portal as gear icon.

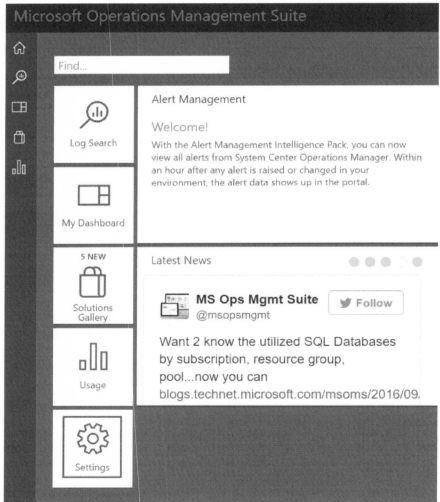

In Settings, go to the Connected Sources -> Windows Servers. Note the Workspace ID and the Primary Key as shown below:

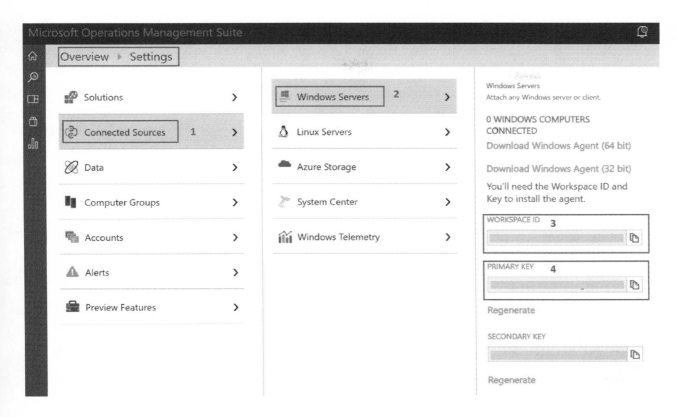

ARM Template Sections for OMS integration

Within the VM resource, you need to define the OMS extension as shown below:

```
"resources": [
{
"type": "extensions",
"name": "Microsoft.EnterpriseCloud.Monitoring",
"apiVersion": "[variables('apiVersion')]",
"location": "[resourceGroup().location]",
"dependsOn": [
"[concat('Microsoft.Compute/virtualMachines/', variables('vmName'))]"
],
"properties": {
"publisher": "Microsoft.EnterpriseCloud.Monitoring",
"type": "MicrosoftMonitoringAgent",
"typeHandlerVersion": "1.0",
"autoUpgradeMinorVersion": true,
"settings": {
"workspaceId": "Your Workspace ID Here"
},
"protectedSettings": {
"workspaceKey": "Your Workspace Key Here"
}
}
```

```
      }
   ]
```

The above configures the OMS on the VM. Note that you need the nested extension resource of type "Microsoft.EnterpriseCloud.Monitoring".

Also, note the Workspace Id and Key in the template section above. Enter the values as per your environment which we found in the Prerequisites section above.

Providing the Workspace ID and Workspace Key Dynamically

You can also provide the Workspace Id and the Workspace Key dynamically by only using the OMS Workspace name. Follow the below sample. Note the use of reference, listKeys, and resourceId helper functions.

```
"settings": {
"workspaceId": "[reference(resourceId('Microsoft.OperationalInsights/workspaces/', parameters('workspaceName')), '2015-0
3-20').customerId]"
},
"protectedSettings": {
"workspaceKey": "[listKeys(resourceId('Microsoft.OperationalInsights/workspaces/', parameters('workspaceName')), '2015-
03-20').primarySharedKey]"
}
```

Reference: You can check the complete quick starter template for OMS integration here: GitHub Sample - Deployment of a Windows VM with OMS Extension

CHAPTER 15 - CREATING ARM TEMPLATE FROM AN EXISTING AZURE INFRASTRUCTURE AND MODIFYING IT

Jumpstarting the ARM Template Development

When developing ARM Templates you do not need to write the template from scratch. You can create ARM Template from an existing similar deployment in Azure.

This chapter is for you if:

- You want to backup an Infrastructure configuration/setup in Azure and want to redeploy it to another environment then this chapter is for you.
- You want to create similar infrastructure as one of the existing deployments in Azure
- You want to modify the configurations of existing Azure IaaS infrastructure and redeploy various elements

This **Power Tip** is really easy if you know just the option.

1. If you want to make the template for all the resources in a Resource Group in Azure, then go to the properties of the Resource Group and find the option for "**Automation Script**".
2. If you want to get the template only for a particular resource, then navigate to that resource in the Azure Portal and then open its settings. You will find the same "**Automation Script**" option.

You can check this option in the below screenshot.

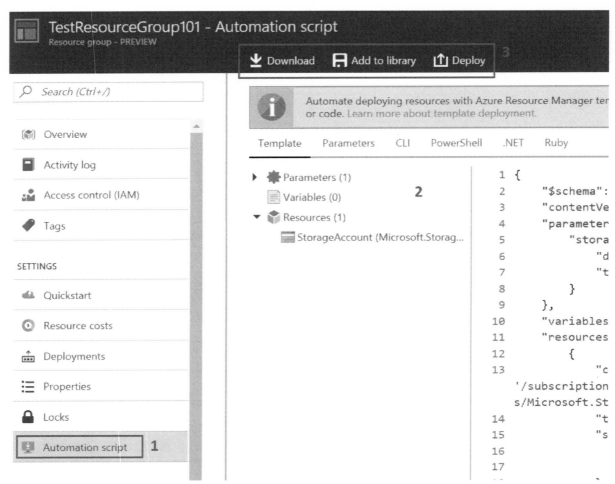

Once you click on the Automation Script option in the settings (of a resource group or a resource) then you will be presented with the complete JSON template along with the JSON outline on the right side (marked 2 above in the image).

You have various options for the actions to take on the template (marked 3 in the image above):

- You can download the template
- Add to Library to deploy the same resources again and again in your subscription
- To directly deploy the resources again with the modifications you make.

Normally, you would download the template to make edits to the same. After downloading, you should start cleaning up the template. There are only 4 major tasks that you need to perform as part of the cleanup:

1. Remove any **hard-coded values** for various dependent resources e.g. NIC for a VM, VHD for a VM etc.
2. Remove any resources and dependent parameters that you don't need.
3. Create **Parameters** for the values you want to change for each deployment and want the end user to provide during the deployment.
4. Create **Variables** for the values which can have fixed values but are being used at multiple locations in your template.

That's all there is to it. Using this tip you can spearhead your ARM Template developments. You don't need to start from scratch and can base your templates on the existing deployments.

IN CONCLUSION

This book in no way covers all the topics that are related to ARM Templates. There are lot more concepts that you can learn as you develop more and more ARM Templates. But the objective of the book is to have you on the ground and working on ARM Templates with best practices in a practical way. By now you should feel comfortable in development of ARM Templates. Book covers the essential features which you will need 95% of the time.

If there are any additional topics you want to see in this book please let us know and I will strive to provide updates on any important content.